TO BLOOM IN THE VALLEY

by

KAMILLE ELIZABETH GRAHAM

Published By: Books By KJF, LLC
https://www.booksbykjf.com
ISBN: (Hardback) 979-8-9917571-0-2
ISBN: (Paperback) 979-8-9917571-1-9
ISBN: (EBook) 979-8-9917571-2-6
ISBN: (Audiobook) 979-8-9917571-3-3

Library of Congress Control Number:
2024926979

Editor: Darian Neely
Cover Photograph/Cover Design by: Noemi Defeo

First Edition
Country of printing:
United States

BOOKS BY KJF

"Everyone has a book on the inside of them waiting to be discovered."

DEDICATION

To the ones who dare to water the seeds in yourselves and others, no matter how small the seedling may be. I pray your flowers bloom from your darkest places.

TABLE OF CONTENTS

III.   FLOWERING

PART 1: SPROUT

NO VACANCY

Breathing from my soul
It seems like I have nowhere else to go,
but inside myself,
which is scarier than a haunted house.
More terrifying than the deepest woods at
midnight.
You're afraid to turn around.
You don't know what's out there.
The floor creaks with every step as
I stumble down the halls of my conscience.
I wish I could say I knew where I was going,
but for this, there is no GPS.
The slightest wind pulls me in a different
direction;
I'm at a loss for words.
The only thing I can gain is insight
and some pain.
The pain parades as wisdom
wise beyond my age.
"Girl, you so smart!"
seems like the only thing they have to say.
Or, not to mention
"You got hips for days."
"Your life seems so perfect!"
Really? Thanks.
No really, thank you
because comments like that
keep you and me from seeing
the other side.

If you saw that side,
then those compliments would cease.
If you are mesmerized by how ornate the
door is, then you may not try to open it.
I would miss those compliments, because
they're the only thing keeping me at ease.

ROOTS/VIEWS FROM THE TREE

If our roots were visible, it would be so
much harder to judge others.
We could see exactly what we're being fed
and identify every knot in the root keeping
us from receiving love properly.
We'd have to lay it all on the table.

If our roots were visible,
then we'd see the beauty in decaying leaves.
We'd see everyone for who they are
underneath all the flowers and
pulchritudinous things.
Things God sees.
The sanctification of the Son uproots every
bad seed.

Everything in nature has a process, but the
Spirit has its own flavor.
Nature says, "death is the end,"
but Jesus's death is our beginning of life.
Like decay buried in the soil provides
nutrients for new life, the Son of Man died
so that we could bloom.

Free from the confines to perform like
flowers, we can just be.
The freedom to know that living water feeds
our roots daily and the fruit gets sweeter day
by day.
If only our roots were visible,

we'd see the twists,
the turns,
the backwards and sideways maze that
comprises our lives.
If only roots were visible,
we'd see
the thumbprint of God.

FREESTYLE/LIKE A CHILD AGAIN

Freestyle
Like a child again
The innocence
The joy
The beauty
The authenticity
When we try to be
no one other than who we were
created to be

Purpose sealed in promise
Delivered at the hands of the Messenger
himself
With the best message of all
Our freedom

How many times has He been denied?
Demonized?
How many times has the rooster crowed in
our own lives?
How many new mornings have we had to
walk with Love again?

Endless are these mercies that hold my heart
nearer than my next word
The Living Word
But unlike us, He doesn't demand to be
heard.
He sends the message on the wind and prays
that we lean in

to His soft whisper of Grace.
Just like His pursuit and the wind, it is
impossible to escape, even when we face the
other way.

BROKEN PUZZLE PIECE

I would ask you to be patient with my
pieces,
but I'm not sure if you'll like the picture
when the puzzle is complete.
I'm happier being broken.
I don't want anyone to fix me.
I'm sorry I made you think you were
working towards something.
I'm working towards getting Christmas gifts
and not having people think I'm a mess.
I'll make everyone happy one day.
I'll be picture perfect one day.
My pieces won't fit every puzzle and forcing
it will only make my ends fragile.
Yes, I'm fragile.
I can't cry though.
I can't complain because honestly,
nothing is really wrong.
I wish I could tell you everything about me,
then erase it from your mind,
and maybe you'll love me again
without pity or remorse.
Don't baby me, baby,
because my mentality is more of a demented
old person who's preparing to forget
everything, including their very identity.
I can't forget what I never learned.
I can only remember what I've formulated in
my imagination, but I've lied to myself more
than once.

I've tried to fit pieces where they don't belong.
I've tried to fit love where it didn't belong.
I've tried to make sense of things, and I only counted ones, ones who didn't care about me, but tried everything in their power to pretend to.

'SHE GOT THAT GOOD HAIR'
Grab me by my roots and pull me hard.
Manipulate me like I do my dolls,
but be gentle please.
Each tear and rip remind me why I'm never
safe.
Wars have started over this mane.

I grew up wanting my hair to be my princess
crown,
Long and straight
Each strand perfection to its finest.

War cries in the fight to be the prettiest
Trauma
I jump at the sight of a hot comb
and shame comes close to my scalp again.
Singe my roots and remind me again why
I'll never be perfect?

Maybe, just maybe I can get the perfect curl
effortlessly,
but coils and kinks always crawl their way
under my skin and come out of every pore.
Remind me again why I'll never be perfect?

"She's got good hair, I want hair like hers"
If we're judging based on behavior
My tresses got an F,

never uniform, doesn't follow gravity's
rules, always fighting against any
manipulation.
Remind me again why I'll never be perfect?

I have a toxic relationship with heat.
He leaves me damaged to the point where I
can't go back to my natural state
but I always go back for more
knowing it'll hurt me in the end.
I'm dedicated to developing my kinks
but let me just check quickly and see how
much we've grown.

RIBCAGE
Tina Turner asked, "what's love got to do
with it?"
I don't know
what love has to do with the material things
under the Christmas tree wrapped in bows,
or what love has to do with a beating heart
in a chest wrapped in veins.
Some people say love is the reason it still
beats,
but this is not a love poem.
This is a warning.

When my heart sinks, I can pull it back to
surface,
but when it flutters, I'm afraid it'll fly away,
and I'll never catch it again.

It's trapped in a ribcage I can't open yet but
maybe that's good.
From inside that cage is the only way I can
feel anything.

There's no CPR for a heart broken by love.
There's only "make a decision and move
on."
So don't put yourself in a place where you
need saving,
unless you're ready to leave your heart
where you leave your love.

Is your heart the princess waiting to be
saved or the monster locked away to keep
everybody else safe because you love too
hard?
This is not a love poem.
This is a warning.
Your heart is in a cage for a reason.

DEPRESSION

Not being able to laugh at a joke
you thought was hilarious before--
that's what depression feels like.
Knowing that pain is inevitable is one thing.
Feeling it all the time is another.
So many people see depression as some sad,
rainy day feeling.
It's more than that.
It's tears one day,
numbness the next.
It's a clouded mind
with heartache and suffering,
you have no control over when the overcast
lifts.
It's that feeling when you care
so much,
but not at all.
It's that feeling when you have a mind full of
dreams,
but not a single care to chase them.
Not because you can't,
but because you don't see the purpose.
You're just gonna die someday anyway,
right?
Depression is the feeling when you don't
want to get out of bed in the morning
because although you know you have a
wonderful day ahead,
you know it's going to be dreadful in your
head.

LAMENTATIONS REMIX

What type of good God would let me feel
this way?
I mean even an earthly father would at least
hold his daughter if he saw her crying like
this.
Maybe I didn't do enough good works
today.
Maybe He's reserved His affections for
those that actually seek Him, and He'll
handle their problems first because my
seniority rank is lacking.
They keep talking about this good Shepherd
and these testimonies,
but I'll be honest--my list of testimonies is
slacking.
If this was service, I'd have to think a little
bit before I had something to say
because right now, all it seems I can
perceive is pain
Logically, this pain indicates no Savior
And passerbys would retort "Jesus who?" if
they saw my behavior.

My heart cries out for a God I feel I'm not
worthy of.
I'm at this crossroads of resolve,
Reaching out for a touch of the same Father
who others have told me to be fearful of lest
He disown me.
I mean, really?

19

I don't know to bow or hug
How do I both give and receive my
inheritance?
It seems as though I've been relegated to a
quarter of a servant as others comment about
how their Father rewards them with full
adornment.
When will it be my time for such comfort?
When will I be able to relinquish my cares
into my Father's arms and let go, finally not
be tense,
thinking if I make one wrong move I could
slip out of His grasp at any moment?

I've heard so many praises of the God of
justice but the loving God the Father who
wipes tears away appears silent
as far away as the sorrowful night is to the
joyous morning.
I finally contend with what caused Jeremiah
to lament.

ROCK, THE CHURCH

I don't know about you but when I first
started walking with the Lord
I wanted to walk like Peter.
I wanted to walk on water.
I was like, "Jesus I'm ready!"
And He said "Come."

Excited, I started out of the boat
but the voices of the others began to drown
my Lord's simple command.
"Do you know if the water is safe?"
"What is your Plan B just in case?"

I was willing to walk on water until the
water reminded me of home no longer.
I was willing to give up my boat until I was
reminded I'd have nothing if this failed.
I would rather my security than my Savior.
There are people who doubt He's real
anyway
but apparently nobody thought to question
why taxes are necessary.

He who sows sparingly reaps sparingly.
A tithe means giving to God the first fruit of
your income
but I'm not really driven to giving when I
see the bill on my table for more money than
what's in my pocket and then I see this

luxury car and designer that pastor is
rocking.
For faith the size of a mustard seed, they
must know some undisclosed planting
technique.

It looks easy to step out on the water and
follow God until the wind starts blowing.
I know the winds obey Him and all, but
would He even speak to them for me?
My footing was great until the waves started
flowing and splashing saltiness in my face.

I resolved to becoming salty with it,
resting back into the shackles of doubt until
the chain-breaking grace started to cause this
confinement to shake.

I'll trade my confusion for bliss.
I fear I'll give up all to temptation because I
honestly don't have enough willpower to
resist.
Yet God's perfect will empowers me to
contend
for the Faith
despite the rocky waves
and occasional doubt.

On Faith, I will be established when the
friction won't relent.

Despite all reason, like the Apostle, I will
live my life sent.

I resolve to remain free
even when it doesn't add up and all of the
odds are against me.

BREAKTHROUGH

Growing upward is the most difficult motion
when your past
and people of it
want to hold you down
and shame you for trying to grow.
I outgrew my own promises
but I am not sorry.
I can't confine myself to one belief when I'm
trying to grow
or to people that will hold it against me.
When my mind changes,
the things I'm asking for will too.
No, I never lied to you
what I said, I truly believed.
Now I think differently.
When God gives me seeds,
I am determined to water them.
If I choose to leave,
I refuse to let those past thoughts haunt me.

DEAR NO ONE
Dear No One,
if our relationship is anything like my
relationship with writing,
I hate you
but I love you, I love you, I love you
One for the pen
One for the paper
One for the spirit
This is far from toxic.
I love more than the idea of you
than the feel of you
Baby, I just love you.
This eternal promise is stronger than any
marriage
The ring being the circle of life
that I can't escape,
not that I would want to.
No matter how far I go away from you,
I promise I'll always return.
Please don't ever forget me
because you never leave my mind.
You are my mind
and every twisted idea that somersaults
across it.
Minor damage,
the heat of this fire left third degree burns
and I'm still shedding my skin
raw.
The rawest thing I could ask for is you.

The rawest thing I could fathom is one-third
of you
because I could never imagine your capacity
in its entirety
and I'm scared that if I ever did, I won't
come back from it
because this is it.
In my dying breath, I'll be ever thankful I
found you.
I kept you.
I held onto you like my life depended on it,
it did.
Those nights you saved me from myself.
Those nights you forced me to name things
and faces I wanted to forget
and you were always one step ahead.
I could trust fall into your arms
and there was never a time you wouldn't
hold me, even when I begged you to let go.
I will never outgrow you.
I will never worry about you not meeting my
standards
because the Lord gave me this gift and I
pray,
with this, we can one day meet His.
You express yourself to me in a way that I
always understand too well.
Communication is key
And the lock
And the door

that I'm forever trying to break down
between my thoughts and this world.
You exist in this world
but in mind as well.
If only you were human
After all, maybe I don't want you to be.
I'm flawed.

THE SMART GIRLS' STRUGGLE

You abandoned me. You told me "You're
gonna be something great one day!" and left
me to figure out how.
For everything I've been through on my
own, I can't tell if it's been by choice.
For everything I've been through on my
own, I can't tell if it's been made worse by
my refusal to open up.
Of course, if I ever opened my mouth to
recite any negative feelings,
I'd be met with, "You're too smart for that,
for him,
for her,
for your own good."
For every time I've been told to get out of
my head,
you would think I boarded up the windows
with an eviction notice on the door.
My mind isn't always comfortable.
On the weekends, I like to take vacations in
other people's problems just to avoid my
own.
Every now and then, after Spring cleaning, I
find those positive words and prayers stored
in the back room.
Please don't come knocking on my front
door.
I promise I won't answer
until it's tidy enough for you
until I get my thoughts together.

Trying to rile my thoughts is like trying to
rile a bunch of carrier pigeons, all with
different messages.
And when I'm lucky enough to get them
together and share them with you,
they'll fly right over your head.

COLLEGE APPLICATION THE POEM

I don't fit into college applications.
Sure, I make good grades, but there are so
much more to me than A's.
What application is accurate if they don't ask
me my favorite color?
Or the thoughts that run through my head at
night?
Or whose hand I think fits most comfortably
in mine?
I personally believe they're afraid of the
answer.
It might not fit their criteria.
They might not have enough room for me to
describe why maroon is my favorite color,
but not too much red and not too much
purple.
Only in the right tint,
they only want me if I'm the right tint.
It doesn't matter what my grades are,
if they look better on her.
I like to believe colleges use applications to
pick and choose their favorite parts
to build their ideal student,
only letting in the parts that are necessary.
Like its heart,
the one who did the most community
service.
Like its brain,
the one who made straight A's.

They don't mind leaving out the other
things.
Like its tongue,
the one who's willing to speak out for things
in which they believe.
Speak,
but not too much.
Think,
but not too much.
Let us train your mind and mold you into the
person we want you to be.
Ignore those thoughts that tell you this isn't
you.
That cap and gown isn't you.
That doctorate degree isn't you.
You're a high school diploma and a
successful small business.
You deserve more credit than you get
for the work you put in to please what others
want you to be.
Don't worry if you're failing one or two
classes.
You're passing the most important one—
being yourself
and the only prerequisite for this class
is living authentically.

LIKE MOTHER, LIKE DAUGHTER

Like Mother, Like Daughter
The sins of a mother,
or so one would say.
She gives you her love,
but also her pain.
It burdens your heart
to know of such sadness
that you gave.
So you try so hard to save
her from her pain,
your pain.
Even after she's gone,
it'll still live with you.
The chain never ends.
The sins of your mother
become the sins of your own,
the sins of your daughter.

FRUIT OF THE WOMB

I wonder what that time was like for God
and Eve before He introduced her to Adam.
I wonder if she said nothing but marveled at
the creation of her Lord before He assigned
Adam as her lord.
Was Sarah there as Abraham was promised
inheritance
to be the father of many nations?

I imagine the promises of God are not split
equally but made separately,
the inheritance of man to crush the head of
the serpent and
God chose us women to be His hand
in the earth.
To carry
a paintbrush in our wombs
To create
fruit,
full communities,
a nation,
Salvation that is pure.
"Let it be to me according to your word."

Among the mysteries of God's creation is
the woman.
As creation groans and we cry out in labor
pains
with expectancy,
even in the push, our weakness is strength.

Our painful moments are the birthing tables
for new strength.
The God who gives power to the faint and
increases strength to those who have no
might
will surely provide.

Perhaps the 'weaker vessel' is a canvas for
the strength of God to be made even more
manifest.
With one foot in the grave and one foot in
Heaven,
we have what it takes to create.

Created for the sweetest of communion with
our Creator,
Who answers our questions with an intuitive
mind,
made us women a physical manifestation
Of His hand
in creating mankind.
Open wombs to only be filled by the One for
which they were created,
the image of the consummate,
you know what I'm saying?

It's in vulnerability that God is invited in
more deeply
and there He wants to dwell with us,
a sacrifice of ourselves
to bear more fruit for all mankind.

34

MIRACLE BABY

They say that the two most important days
in someone's life are the day they are born
and the day they figure out why.
"I'm ready!
I'm ready!!
Put me in this earth now!
No, it's not too early!
I'm gonna make it!
I see so much in my future, I'm gonna make
it!
Your lies can't stop me!
Your abuse can't stop me!
Nothing can stop me!
God said I would be here
and I'm here!
He will use me in a mighty way!"

My spirit cried this from before I was born
weighing only 1 pound and 15 ounces.
When doctors said I wouldn't make it,
the Spirit of God rose from within me and
freed me from the breathing tubes,
from the fear,
from the abuse,
from the lies,
from the depression,
from the addiction,
for His magnification,
for His glory.

God of my creation,
God of my salvation,
I'm sorry if I ever thought for a moment that
You wouldn't fulfill Your purpose in me
or that I didn't have one.
How silly of me to think that You performed
a miracle to put me here and not for a
purpose?
How great you are Lord
At 25 and a half weeks gestation you said
"It's time."
You said, "I want her here and I want her
here now."
You said, "Your purpose starts now."
At 12, when depression tried to take back
what You birthed,
At 18, when depression tried to take back
what You birthed,
You said, "I want her here and I want her
here now."
You said, "Your purpose starts now."

PART 2: SEEDLING

THE SPACE BETWEEN

I swear on a poem
That my decisions will be imperfect, to a
fault.
My words are timeless,
buried under metaphors, cliches, and
beautiful phrases,
especially when my mortal body comes in
contact with celestial bodies,
and just for a second, I think I'm flying.
I'm flawed to a fault,
writing beautiful words all over my soul,
hoping that just for one moment
I can disguise my humanity.
I can talk my way through pain.
I can write my way through calamity,
but when the veil comes down
and I face my truth at the altar,
I hope someone speaks, because I don't
know how much longer I can hold my
peace.
I hope someone says that they know the real
me,
that they've finally figured out how to
untangle all the cords, making connections
in my head.
I hope they've broken down the barrier
between what I know and what I feel.
I hope they've figured out how to articulate
my tongues of other planets.

But until then, I'll be a pathway
between thinking, feeling, and being,
always standing on one side more than the
other,
between Earth and other dimensions,
between imperfection and realization.

STREAM OF CONSCIOUSNESS/BEING IN LOVE

I had no intentions to catch feelings.
As love would have it,
I did.
I am a love driven person, drawing
inspiration from the love that overflows
from the hearts of others and not their
overflow in bank accounts.
Nothing makes me happier than putting a
smile on others' faces.
Wisdom from years I haven't lived,
and love in response to versions of people I
have yet to meet.
Purpose,
a version of her
that I can't quite see but still aim to be
and catch glimpses of her in passion,
in writing,
in living,
in loving and being loved.
In thinking
self to self,
a narrative not many would understand but
are dying to read
and dissect as if they could ever understand
the rules of this language.
A conglomerate of all my experiences
and my personal commentary for
processing,
bathed and coated in scripture,

but by comparison
not clean enough to remove the dirt that
builds character.
Lotus flower,
beauty grown from the earth's worse,
but I reckon that human filth stinks more,
erodes.
So perhaps I shouldn't be so moved by the
passing waste of man
that repulses those around it from
a ten-foot distance.

I'm so glad that grace travels farther than ten
feet
and moves faster than my ability to
overthink whatever I am about to say.
Word vomit,
oopsies,
but the true artist is able to make priceless
art from priceless items.

I applaud the one who can follow and make
sense of my stream of consciousness
and even more the One who created it and
completes it.
No matter how many times I daily detour
from the objective path,
it somehow still never steps outside of the
parameters of purposeful life.
I have yet to figure out if I have purpose or
am purpose myself,

lost in a realm of thought, throwing a
fishline to anyone willing to catch it and
solve,
to resolve,
to understand my personhood and walk with
me as I learn to understand it myself.
Maybe this is what it truly means to be in
love.
I had no intentions to catch feelings,
but after all, who does?

DARKEST PERSON IN THE ROOM

Today, I realized something.
I was the darkest person in the room
and I didn't have a choice in the matter.
I couldn't decide whether or not I wanted it
to be like that.
No matter what I wanted, it was still going
to be that way.
My only option was to walk out
to make it so that it wasn't so,
but in doing so, I forfeit their experience
and jeopardize my budding image.
So, I had to be okay with it.
Not for myself
but so I could thank my future self
and my pride.
But I wasn't okay with it,
still not okay with it
and it's never going to be what I make it.
I had to learn to adjust my definition of okay
or if I don't,
I'll constantly be
in a state of discomfort.
So, I have to get used to
the new and strange feeling
of the warmth of my melanin
Radiating
with waves of light
and heat
with a force
for which they were not ready.

THORN I
Even the prettiest flowers
As delicate and sensitive as their facade
If you get too close,
We can still damage you
I really wish love didn't hurt sometimes
I really wish love didn't force sometimes
Oh wait
Love doesn't force
But I force my agenda in the name of love
I'm sorry
Thorn.

I regret thinking love was something that
would leave a stain,
When true Love washes away stains
Crimson to clean
But the wolves of my past that masqueraded
as lovers
Did not hesitate to leave bite marks.
Maybe that's why I think love bites are
somehow affection,
Thorn.

I tried hard not to write another love poem,
But my consciousness somehow always
romanticizes love turned pain
Pain turned love
Thorn.

Love took all the pain that we deserved,

So why do I still have this
Thorn?
Why do I still daydream about selfish love,
About aggressive love,
But not love love
When I know Love?
Thorn.

So why do I still accept worldly love when I
know it's not real?
Worldly love didn't die for me, but expects
me to die for it.
So why am I so quick to lay my heart down,
To lay down with selfish love
And accept it.
Too weak to say no, too strong to let it go.
Thorn.

I'm working on that
Love is working on that
Because as Paul said
Even with this thorn in my side,
His grace is sufficient.
So even with this thorn in my side,
I will still praise You.
I'll still praise my Savior
Because every thorn we'll ever have
The Savior adorned in a crown on His head
So, I'll praise Him.

THORN II

St. Paul said "I was given a thorn in my
flesh, a messenger from Satan to torment me
and keep me from becoming proud. Three
times I begged the Lord to remove it but He
said my grace is sufficient for you, My
power is made perfect in your weakness"

—-

I don't know about you, but I'm in an
abusive relationship with Target.
Meaning every time I go into Target, they
tell me what to buy even though I already
told myself I was only getting salad, but I
digress.
The other day I went into Target and Target
told me to buy some beautiful dark pink
roses with baby breath and make myself a
bouquet!
So I did
As I'm pruning and preparing this beautiful
display for my home,
The excitement leaps out of me in the form
of pain as my finger brushes the thorns
Painful, but beautiful
More beautiful maybe because God the
Creator determined their worth
Knew we would value the roses and covet to
keep them for ourselves
And protected them in the form of their
thorns
And we deem them beautiful still

A famous rapper once said there's beauty in
the struggle
And gladly I'll bleed for the beauty of these
here roses on display
Thorns and all
But do I dare bleed for the beauty of my
own display
Even the thorns I hate...
The dichotomy between pain and beauty is
something many of us women know very
well.
I had caterpillars for eyebrows growing up,
So around 10 or 11 when I first started
getting them arched, I fully expected the
pain to accompany the beauty coming
Becoming
But what I didn't expect
Was that pain and beauty would become
best friends for the rest of my life
So around 10 or 11 when my eyes were first
opened to the dark shadows of depression, I
expected it to be a passing visitor
But it stayed
As I grew, this shadow seemed to grow with
me
As I learned and experienced the beauty of
life, the pain was sure to remind me of its
presence
This thorn.
I'm a feeler
what I feel is magnified, the good and bad

Knowing me, I'll make it find meaning
Even if it means very little in the grand
scheme of things
Those little things mean something
It is the details of life where we can get lost
but also in these details, we find the
profound
We know the rose is worthy to be found, but
maybe the thorn is too.
The plane of this Earth has a way of
contorting our vision
To where we see the thorn before the rose
The pain before the beauty
And we discount it as not beautiful at all
But who throws the whole rose away
because of the thorn?

IG FILTER THE POEM
How much time do we spend
on our timelines thinking
"She is so beautiful"
"I love their relationship"?
But she cries herself to sleep at night and
they have been through so much that 1
million people can't count it on 10 million
fingers.
What you see is what you get.
I think I do good for someone with trust
issues
I always trust what everyone posts on social
media as the life they live
The things they enjoy
I envy
the pain they endure
I envy their pain and their ability to hide it
from anyone not looking closely enough
What pain?
What insecurities?
What relationship problems?
They don't exist in the realm of being
completely honest
And I'm gonna be completely honest
I envy myself
What I show of me, the perfection I want
others to believe exists
I envy the person that other people think I
am
Because I am

So much more
I possess external beauty, yes
But there are museums to behold in my
conscience
if you have the right access.
I am my intelligence, sure
But I am also my exaggeration and
boringness and irrelevancy and overthinking
and rambling and
never getting straight to the point.
And I'm going to get straight to the point
Let's be real
I have layers to expose
And I'm inviting you to be real with me
Or we'll be fake together
either way.
Remove the mask because we need to agree
I can be raw when everyone else has peeled
off their layers.

DEAR EMPATHS
For all my empaths out there…

Disillusioned
I'm tired of people seeing me but not really
seeing me.
I'm tired of begging people to care enough
to dissect the layers I expose before them.
I'm tired of expecting me from people who
are not me.
I'm tired of always understanding yet not
being understood.

Disenchanted
I'm tired of being taken as the prop of a con
artist.
I'm tired of people touching my soul just to
get a kick out of it.
Not considering how fragile of a state it is
in,
Then blame me for bearing these wounds.
I should've known better.
I should've done better.

Dismayed
How did I so unsuspectingly allow others to
hijack what was dearest to me?
How did broken glass and broken dreams
leave me with less questions and not more?
How did this backwards and messed up path
lead to peace?

Now
Do the friends that I have call themselves
that?
Do they speak positively of me behind my
back?
Has my trauma finally allowed me the
comfort of experiencing how I feel to the
extent that I don't care about how others feel
about how I feel?
Yet
Here we are
Yet again caring how others feel
Do I even have to say it?
I will.

Sweet empath…
What would you do for love?
Honey,
How many times has love soured and you
tried to make it sweet again?
How many times has the love you had been
lost,
And you seem to be the only one who cares
enough to pick up the pieces along the way
and gently place them in the lost and found
in case their owner returns for them again?
What has this done for you?
Except make you more aware and by
spiteful habit still less selfish.
You become a culmination of your habits.

Stop lying to yourself, everything you do,
you exude care.
Maybe you don't care,
Maybe you are care.
And as you would with anything else this
precious,
With yourself
Please, I beg you, be delicate.

NAKED AND ASHAMED

The shame is not mine.
Ten years of carrying someone else's
baggage for me to realize the weight
No matter how much I care for them, their
lack of regard for my yet developing purity
was enough for me to backseat the
compassion and put my own protection
behind the wheel.
My identity was rocked by this ordeal
Years later, still picking up the pieces of
who God said I was before this happened to
me,
And the redemption of who I am still.
The resurrection of purity that was once
dead to my soul is beginning to untie its
grave clothes
And man, I'm glad about it.

Is it possible to be both Martha and Lazarus?
Wishing Jesus had just come earlier
Mourning the death of what I thought was
formally dead,
my innocence,
yet patiently waiting for the Resurrection to
come untie from this bondage
To seal my own tomb, and feel as though no
one would weep for me
Jesus wept.

The very One who would eventually say rise
is the only One who fully grieved the part of
me that had died.
It speaks volumes of my identity if I'm the
reason the Savior cried
when I was unbelieving
that based on what I've seen, I could be
living and fully revived.

The exposure to someone else's demons
when I had not yet grown into my own faith
to shield me,
Wielding weapons of mass insecurity to
protect me from the thought that someone
could actually love me
Without me having to do anything for them.

You can shame me all you want
But the shame is not mine to carry.
So, to my abusers,
as polite as I may be
No.
I will not carry your baggage for you.

TODAY'S ROSA PARKS

Today, you can't have my seat
without asking.
If I have to explain why you shouldn't be
taking it without consent,
That's an issue of your entitlement.
Just because you've been entitled to this
earth throughout history
does not mean you are
Right now
Entitled to my voice.
You are not entitled to hear my "no"
As a "maybe"
As a "try harder"
And you are not allowed to keep trying
Our Me Too no is this generation's Rosa
Parks' no.
This time, we're standing
for survivors.
We survivors have been pushed to the back
of the bus too many times
Doubted and lied on
When our truths were as evident as "we
have every right to sit in the front as
everyone else"
We have every right to be believed as
everyone else
And we are reclaiming our seats.
This time,
Just like last,
We won't be moved

Until revolutions break out.
Today, you cannot have my seat
without asking.

DEAR MY FUTURE DAUGHTER

Dear my future daughter,
you are more than your body,
than your lips or your thighs.
You're worth more than sex,
or being that one black friend.
You are your brilliant mind
and the positive energy you spread.
Let your sexuality shine on you,
but not define you.
Boast the melanin in your skin
and how proud you are to wear it.
Know that it comes with problems,
but also an awareness,
a promise to fulfill.
As a woman, society will push you to your
knees
for a man.
Know that you are better than that.
A boyfriend or husband is not your only
priority.
With your smarts, you'll have a world to
save.
Make sure whichever partner you choose
can help you save it.
Fill your loneliness with intelligence and
soulfulness.
Channel your "inner black woman."
Not the one society disregards as obnoxious,
loud, and unnecessary

and definitely not the one of who would've
obeyed
when the slave master told her not to
scream.
But be the one you have to be.
Actually,
Do be the loud, black woman.
Be the one who sets our people free.
Be loud with wisdom,
Be loud with passion,
Be loud with courage and cries for justice,
Be loud with respect
For yourself and for others.

MASTER'S PLAN
Relax honey, it's all part of the master plan.
Are you relaxed?
Okay, now what if I told you it's all part of
the Master's plan?

That the One who created this universe is
the Master of Love?
So somehow
I gotta trust
That all things
will work together
for good
Not that all will be good

Somehow
God recycled this pain and violence against
me
Into art
But He's not new to this

The DNA of the earth is written in cycles
So my goodness
I'm honored when God breaks one for me
It's a cycle
hurt people hurt people
But good God
He broke that cycle and said
Hurt people can love
Harder
He recycled stone into life

And blew a fresh wind
All of nature reflects Him

So breathe
Him in
Be kind to the earth
She is His creation
Be kind to one another
She and he
Are made
In the image and likeness of the Creator
We are all connected
by love
And light

Reduce the hate, Reuse the good memories,
Recycle the pain into art.

SIDE EFFECTS INCLUDE
Racing heart
Shortness of breath
Sweating
If you are experiencing any of these
symptoms,
Please visit your local magician
I mean, clinician

These symptoms are signs of the most
popular contagion in the world:
Fear.
It has been a global pandemic for years
This virus can lay dormant for many years.
People often show no symptoms at all until
under stress
Until everything we've put our trust in
becomes infected
Disconnected
Distanced.

Until our faith is tested
and the results come back negative

This is not a virus that washing our hands or
wearing masks can prevent.

OPEN LETTER TO MY FUTURE SON

I'm scared for you.
I don't know how long I can preserve the
innocence I want you to have.
I need you to have,
Before it's stripped away.
Before they no longer see you as a child,
But rather a target.
Before you can fully understand the reason
they will point a gun at you before they
point love at you.
I will point love at you.
I will constantly remind you
Be who you want to be,
Be educated, or sound 'ignant'
Wear a suit or sag your jeans
Find your black boy joy and do your thing
Be happy
but be careful.
No matter how respectable you are, you'll
still just be a spectacle.
Another young black boy everyone watches
on the news as they are slaughtered.
Please be aware,
Please be educated
And please
Please
Whatever you do,
Be a black boy.
Be a boy.
Hold your innocence for as long as you can.

Because there will come a time when they
try to take the toy and the dream out of your
hand
And replace it with something you never
wanted to be there.
....
Did you hear about the black boy killed by
police this year?
Which one?

RAM IN THE BUSH/OUR ISAAC SACRIFICE

I don't know about you all,
But I don't know how Abraham did it.
God promised Abraham that he would be
the father of many nations, then gon' turn
around and tell him to sacrifice his only son.

I can imagine the concern
I can imagine Abraham's conversation with God sounded
a lot like our conversations with God that
sometimes go a little like:

"Lord please, grant me this promise
This gift
And when I get it
When I get it, I'll praise you"

"Okay...why are you taking so long, God?
Forget it
I'm gonna go do it myself!"

"Well, that didn't work out well...God?"

"Lord you're so good! God Almighty there's
nothing you can't do!"

"You want me to do what, God?!
But you just gave me this gift, now you want
me to give it back to You?!"

65

And that's our dilemma
Many times, we sound just like Abraham
Same questions
But do we give the same answers?
God can only bless what we surrender to
Him
But do you want to know the secret?
God already promised Abraham generations
And it is impossible for God to break His
promises
So, Abraham might've already known that
God had to make a way.
But do we stand up and walk with that
promise?
Or hoard and refuse to surrender our "yes"?
Our only begotten son,
Will we give it up?

My God
We struggle with something that God has
already done.
We ask a God who sacrificed his only son
So let go of your Issac sacrifice so that
Jesus's sacrifice can reign.

GREATNESS/MY LAND

To be from the land is not to be one with the
land
Let me rephrase

Only the indigenous believe in "finders
keepers"
As in America's elementary days
When brown skin was dismissed and ripped
away
Because a certain group of people didn't
want to be outnumbered
They coined the term "minority"
And made them us
Because Lord forbid it's ever "we"
Because then there would be what some call
unity
What I call peace
What I call blackness without the subscript
What I call the opposite of a stereotype
Greatness
What I call "I don't have to explain myself
when I walk in the room, you just know, and
already expected it of me."
Greatness
The only byproduct of hope that matters.
Greatness
The reason hope even exists in the first
place.

Great God.

It is in your image we are all made.
Help us to see the Greatness in one another
before anything else.
Selah.

PART 3: FLOWERING

TRY, TRY AGAIN
So I got a question
The same Sun that shines on us today, is it
the same Sun that shone on us when we
were slaves?
After all the things it's seen, it still rises
each day.
After all the trauma I've seen, I ought to rise
with it
I ought to shine with it.

I have heavy clouds over me
So, no wonder
Like rain,
I cry easily
like a newborn first introduced to pain
I mean, life.
Disappointment shocks my nervous system.
"You mean to tell me I came all this way for
this???
Man, earth is ghetto…"
But since we're here we might as well make
something of it right?
We might as well be makers ourselves,
right?

For the love of all

Like nature, we might as well
photosynthesize
Take what's inside of us

And create, produce
Light that gives life
Let me take the light and darkness I've seen,
Stir it inside of me,
And chloro-fill you up with what I've turned
it into.
You see,

It's natural to me
I'm in my element
Like Au
You'll be in awe of this gold buried in me

Some would call it luck that we can do this
Turn trauma into triumph
Create and recreate

Lady Luck

Like a leprechaun
Queen
Black woman
You drip a little gold wherever you go
Black man
You be King
Midas well
Everything you touch turns to gold
You see
It's really a powerful combo I might add

The way light and life go hand in hand,

But we can't always control when it's dark
and rainy
So, we stand
tall until the sun rises again

No matter how many clouds may be
blocking our view,
All we can do is try
Everyday
Some days the Sun will shine through,
and some days not so much but guess what?

Because the Sun says so.

We have another opportunity
To shine
Again
To try
As long as the Sun still rises, so will you and
I.

I GUESS THIS WAS A LOVE POEM

Your smile is more like a reminder why I'm here.
It doesn't light up my world;
It finger paints my world with messy patterns and flows like a river through my heart valves.
Your smile is like blood,
But not the blood that coats the concrete after a horror scene.
More like the blood accompanied by a smile with a huge battle scar that lets the soldier know why they fought.
And your frown,
that ticking time grenade that rolled right in front of me.
I have seconds to find a way to keep it from detonating.
When it's safer to run away, I walk right up to it and enclose it
With love and tenderness to protect the precious destruction.
And oh my god, your laugh.
There is no switch to turn it off and when it still hangs in the air after a good roast session,
that air tastes sweeter than the first time we kissed.
To kiss you, the air is so fresh as if I had just reached the top of a mountain that I'd been climbing for almost seven months.

As much as I want to, I can't move
mountains.
I can't move hurt.
I can't move pain.
I can only climb it and hope when I reach
the top, the fresh air will refill my lungs with
that new type of oxygen unlike any I've ever
inhaled on flat land.

TRIGGER HAPPY

What if I told you,
That when you're about to cry,
That painful lump in your throat
Was only the words you were preparing to throw?

I'm sure my fellow feelers can agree
That sticks and stone pain will go away
And some ointment will alleviate.

But the pain of words,
no band aid can cover, and no apology can erase.
They can be lethal
You would think we would be more careful
with the things we say.

Unforgiveness is ammunition that if we'll be honest, we're all toting
Ready to spew out hateful words when triggered
No gun laws can stop this violence and it's about time we start undressing these wounds
So that we can address these wounds.

Concealed carrying our hearts
Got all of us walking around with our wounds hanging out,
Ready to be infected by the next careless person that doesn't know how to handle us.

But my fault
I didn't tell you it was there
I didn't want to be triggered
I just wanted to shoot
I just wanted to hold you accountable to
every past mistake that someone else made
And call it a standard

Would you still caress me if you knew I was
a loaded gun?
That if you pushed the wrong button or
pulled the wrong switch
That I'd blow?
And what beautiful collateral damage you'd
be.

Truth moment
I'm tired of bleeding on the people around
me
And these wounds only keep opening up no
matter how hard I try to disguise them.

It's time they're treated
It's time they're put in hands so delicate
So trained in treating with patients
I mean, His track record is flawless

Unlike ordinary practitioners
This great Physician is not just practicing
This is His specialty
You are His specialty

With Him it's more about having patience
than it is about being a patient
And there's nothing that you can tell Him
that He's never seen before
His bedside manner is elite
His staff is extremely comforting
His office is always open
I think I heard an old saint say it's called
"Prayer Room."
Something about he writes up all my
prescriptions
He is my primary care provider
I can bear all my wounds before Him and
know they won't be mistreated
for they'll be treated.

I mean you better ask somebody
His reviews are off the charts
Here's something cool
He doesn't need a stethoscope to hear our
hearts.

Oh, and I forgot to mention,
Dr. Jesus does house calls.

CHURCHISM

The law kills, but the Spirit gives life.
I have a PSA to y'all narrow-minded
"church folk,"
And this one might hurt.
The law didn't die for you.
Your knee length skirt and church hat didn't
take the keys from hell for you
Your righteousness most definitely did not
get up out of the grave.
So why do you worship it?

We honor God with our cries of praise, with
our mouths open and our hands lifted
And the last time I checked,
Rocks don't have a dress code.

Before you say it,
I understand modesty
And dressing modestly
I myself do
But before I concerned myself with covering
my knees,
I learned how to cover my household.

I'm not bashing tradition
I can appreciate the praise dances and the
nice clothes,
But I would never put a roadblock to
salvation.

78

Y'all keep telling people about the path they
should be on, not introducing the One who
can lead them to it.
Y'all be
screaming "follow the straight and narrow"
and yet whispering the person of Jesus.
What if I told you your legalism doesn't
make you any different than those who
follow the gay and wide?
I know that hurt your pride
No one is better than anyone.
If any one of us could be perfect, what need
would Jesus have had to die?
The same Jesus loves all humans.
The same Jesus died for all humans.
The same Jesus that we should speak with
daily
that saves souls, to be desired more than
anything.
Yeshua- The only one who is the Fulfillment
of the law that you church folk somehow
think you're good enough to follow.

As humans, we are guaranteed one thing:
we'll never be perfect.
As Christians, we are guaranteed this: He is
perfect in our place.

Perfect love casts out all fear.
So like my Savior, I will love all folks
fearlessly.

I want to live life loving with Jesus,
Before I come to church looking casket
sharp, for the very last time, thinking,
"Finally, perfect."

ELOQUENCE

Our throats are like cages,
Trapping our words,
Leaving us breathless.
Eloquence is choking us.
The need to express our words "eloquently"
Prevents us from expressing them raw and
true.
Our minds are endless production lines
Producing thoughts faster than we can
Comprehend them.
Comprehend what they mean,
The purpose they serve.
Our thoughts are our muse.
The only thing we have on our deathbed
Will we care how eloquently we spoke
them?
Or if we spoke them at all?
Let not your throat be a cage,
Let it be a pathway,
A way to success,
A way to express.
Let what you say,
Not how you say it,
Be your eloquence.

I AM ART AND AN ARTIST
I'm traumatized
But yet, so many seem to have an opinion
about what I should have done differently
Or to invalidate me
But I promise if you had the chance to walk
in my shoes, you couldn't stand it

So, before you go speaking on a situation,
Commenting on my growth,
I want you to just know that I fought
I fought for community
I fought for wealth
I fought for happiness
But pain is just too big of an enemy for me
to fight on my own
Or act like it doesn't exist
Simply because you just don't see it
I'm sick of shelter
It is in nature
God's art
that I feel seen
Baby, I deserve safety.
Artists thrive where they are loved and
appreciated.
The embrace of yesterday
The matrimony of art, love, and life
And freedom to war as I write
And to be a free spirit is to be a free thinker
Expect nothing to come of stifled self-will.
Art flows freely in this realm

I flow freely in this realm
I am art and an artist.
Authenticity and love look good on me.

BRIDE OF CHRIST
Ever since I was a little girl,
I dreamed of being a bride
In a white dress with my Prince Charming
ready to come and sweep me off my feet
A Prince Charming who is madly in love
with me and I with him
Who had a mansion awaiting me and life of
endless love that he had prepared tirelessly
to adorn me with.
I wanted the dream.

As I approached every first
I experienced a failed mimicry of that dream
My first kindergarten boyfriend
My first kiss
My first love
My first soul tie
My first heartbreak
I went through it all still holding firm onto
the piece of dream that has morphed into a
disappointing reality
There was no Prince Charming awaiting me.
I became convinced that I just wasn't
princess enough
Wasn't wife enough to be a bride.
And even the thought of an impure woman
like me in a pure white dress made me feel
like a five-year-old trying on bigger shoes
than I could fill.

I wanted to look the part but knew I'd be
tripping if I tried to walk in it.

As I racked up on disappointments and
failed attempts at achieving my five-year-
old dream,
I stopped seeing myself as Barbie
I stopped believing I could live a Barbie
dream
I stopped believing Prince Charming existed
and that I would never be the centerpiece of
a perfect wedding
I opened my eyes and realized
My own white dress was crimson stained
from all the chasing I'd been doing.
Who would ever want me?
How could I ever be anyone's bride?

I wish I knew then what I know now
That the whole time I was chasing a dream,
That my Prince was just waiting patiently
for me
Since I was five, had grace just for me
I wish I knew then that the only One capable
of loving me eternally had already said I do
He had already made me His beautiful bride
and was pursing me relentlessly
That all of the love that I ever wanted from a
man was in His nail-pierced hands
And He never stopped reaching them out to
me

As I sought attention from others, He was
dying for mine
And it made no difference to Him how pure
I was before Him
Because as His bride, I would be washed
clean and never stained again
I no longer had to don the crimson shame of
my past
I could adorn a pure white dress as He
adorned me with His love forever
He prepared a place for me
A mansion, jewels, and gold streets
Way beyond what I had ever dreamed

No matter how unworthy I thought I seemed
Jesus said, "My beauty you are made clean."
You are not too dirty to be My bride
No matter what others have said about you,
I am unashamed to call you Mine.

I traded Prince Charming for the Prince of
Peace
Once He said, "It is finished"
My love story was complete.

A LOVE AS OLD AS TIME

A love as old as time
Am I stupid for still believing in a love like
this?
Love is the oldest force in the world; am I
wrong to desire love to be the strongest
force in my home?
That sacrificial type of love
The healthy competition kind of love
To see who can love each other harder
Without ever burning out
I have grown accustomed to throwing
myself in the fire to keep others warm,
when their love for me is barely burning in
comparison
A "rider" if you will, but I ain't got no
business being a rider for someone who's
willing to dip out at the first major
inconvenience.
If whatever you sacrifice is more important
than what you gain with me, I'd question
your priorities.
Love at its core is sacrificial,
but there is nothing else on earth
as beneficial.

WHAT, A MAN?
Love is a gift meant to be shared
And by golly y'all, I think I found my
person
This country girl finally has more reasons to
continue loving despite all of the
antagonizing fears and doubts thrust at me
When I'm with him, I feel like the
protagonist, living out the climax of my own
memoir when I realize I'm not too jacked up
to deserve this kind of love
It matters not the narrative others have about
it in their head
This is mine
This is ours
This is tried
This is patient
This is kind

I like the version of myself when she is free
Authenticity
Strength
Flourish most in sensitivity
I like the version of myself when she is
loved properly.
For so long, I was told to love myself to
compensate for those who didn't.
But no one told me how much this sweet
kind of love would make me want to love
myself more.
Man

What a guy

Support is the breeding ground for success
Combined with just the right amount of
enlightenment and depth
These roots baby would surprise you if you
knew how deep they ran

The sensitivity with which he speaks to me
Is the very treasure I begged for before
But this time I don't feel like I'm on
borrowed time,
Waiting on the day he decides I'm not worth
his patience anymore
It seems like he's made of patience
Easy
Overflowing with exactly the understanding
I need
As if his heart was made for me,
Oozing the security that is a woman's desire
as old as time,
I almost feel like we were together even then
Man
What a guy

I never quite understood how people could
say it was love at first sight
But I don't know maybe there's some kind
of connection of the vessels in my heart and
the lines around my smile

Because baby I promise you, I couldn't stop
laughing that night
I finally understand
I've spent so much time in build a man
workshop that I'm learning the freedom of a
ready-made one
I can finally put that time back into myself
as main course with his love as my delicacy
Man
What a guy

He feels like home
So much so that I forgot I don't write love
poems
My views are my own
And the only perspective he's tried to
change of mine is my belief on if I'm
deserving of love
This type of love
Coasts the back roads
And escapades down the city streets
This type of love is versatile
Durable
Can weather the storms of life
And matures beautifully in each season
Every day I find a new reason
to love you
Man.
What. A. Guy.

ROOTED

My grandmother once told me "Sticks and
stones may break my bones but words could
never hurt me."
But let me tell you
her words could build things
like my confidence.
Funny how she could say such a thing,
when her powerful words assembled me.
No wonder why, in my head, I think I'm a
queen
When she would see
a toddling two-year-old and speak over me
"Here comes the Queen
Elizabeth"
Thanks to Jessie and Juanita, I was bred
from royalty.
Dipped in matriarchy and sprinkled with
southern Baptist
Molded my loose clay
Fired me up
Just enough that I would harden
Yet allowed me to remain soft enough to
touch.
I thank you.
For creating me as an original work of art.
Grandma and Papa, you have made a
beautiful family
with us, you have conceived a masterpiece
and signed your names in our genes
We ought to call you Mr. and Mrs. Picasso

You spoke a thing, and it was planted
Now that thing speaks for you
With a voice and a soul built from soil.
Roots deeper than war trenches
Soul ties of wisdom, spiritual ties to the
Word.
Words have broken me, and the Word has
re-sculpted me
No, words cannot hurt
But on the right lips,
they can build up powerhouses
that can withstand
the elements and the test of time
with roots that go way back,
way down to support it.
This boulder has been positioned to make
me stronger.
My grandfather was not always a man of
many words
But when it comes to greatness some things
don't need to be said,
You will just see.
Because of this,
the care with which you've crafted,
I've learned to be comfortable in silence.
These roots run deep and
because they are, I can be.

MATTHEW 12:33
Sometimes
we taste fruit so good we have to ask
"Good Lord, what tree did this come
from?!"
Generations can be fed because of how long
one tree can last.
My great-grandmother is with the Lord, but
many still eat of her fruit.

It's times like this when Annie Bell's
prayers cover me.
When the serpent tries to convince me
that my power is a mirage.
How?
When everyone in my presence sometimes
has to take a step back to take in all this
light?
How could I not walk in Annie Bell's
might?

Generations before me prayed to cover me
and my children's children's offspring.
they know that their produce would be a
commodity.
That when our power is recognized,
they will try to cut us down.

She kneeled to clean after the man, so I can
stand,
eye to eye with the man.

And guess what?
He is intimidated.
Because somewhere deep down, he knows
we have some roots that he don't.
Knowledge, fierceness, and a little bit of
finesse.
The Holy Spirit within me
is becoming.
So, I thank Annie Bell and her warrior
prayers,
for planting a spirit seed.
If I could tell her one thing,
I'd say that the fruit of her labor was well
worth it.

RELATED OR RELATABLE
After years of struggling with my self
esteem,
I can finally say
I think I wanna look like me
Because there's not many features featured
on other faces that I can trace back
generations
And none that are exactly this combination.

I got one of them noses man
My folks said it belonged to my auntie
I found out later it also resided on the
Sphinx
But was destroyed
Because a hater deemed it too much of a
good thing.

I got them cheek bones man
I think it's from my granddaddy's side
Them kinda cheek bones that rise like a high
tide
I can't hide my smile
Even when sorrow and fear tell me I better
shelter it away for safekeeping
I know better than to store a light in a box
where nobody can see it
These cheek bones been rising like a proud
flag blowing in gale force winds for
centuries
So even when the storm comes rolling in,

Ima raise my smile like a banner and say,
"This smile is too expensive, somebody paid
too much for it, for me not to put this here
heirloom on display."

I got them eyes man
Them eyes that bore immense pain but
somehow can still see the beauty in
everything
Maybe it's the astigmatism, right?
That was genetic
The shape of my eyes got me seeing things
that aren't really there
Like their "good intentions"
I'm playing, not really.
But back to the message
They covered our eyes during the Middle
Passage
If we could see, we could find our way
home
But jokes on them, we built a new one and
did it blind.

Even though they're brown and pink I think
these lips are rather fine
With this cute little Cupid bows
In the shape of a heart
The contents of mine spill over the brim of
these here lips.

DNA is a funny thing

How the Creator can take two existing
people and make a brand new being
All of the same and all the way different
It ain't a question of how far the apple fell,
God mighta said "Let me just gon' ahead
and plant a new tree."
I'm thankful for all that I am and all that has
yet to be.
I look forward to a future that has pieces of
me and of those before me yet is something
none of us have ever seen.

LETTER TO LITTLE ME

Hey little girl
Brave little girl
I know I don't speak to you often, but I
really love you
You knew you were different
You just didn't know how strong you were
How strong you are
I'm sorry
For things that were in my control and
things that were not
I'm sorry you were forced to grow up fast
I'm sorry you intimately knew pain before
you had the words to express
But girl
When you found the words, you were
unstoppable
Girl
When you found yourself, you became a
force
I know because it happened last month
Last week
Yesterday
Coming of age is a scary but thrilling thing.
I would be miserable lest I forget about you
What you need
What you want
What excites you
What makes you sad
What inspires you
Do I inspire you?

It's not prideful to admit that my love
You're not prideful by admitting your
greatness my love

I wish I could re-see your thoughts
I wish I could give you the validation you
never got
And that every time you were overwhelmed,
I came in and reminded you that you were
specially designed to carry this
To make light come of this
To make joy come of this
Dare I say others could not manipulate the
same prism enough to reflect the Light that
you do
It's a gift even though you deemed it a curse
for 22 years
The very thing that makes you you.

But let's start treating you like the gift you
are, yeah?

PLAYGROUND OF THE MIND
If ever asked when I leave this earth what I
want to be known for
My words
How they inspire people
How they uplift people
How the words and phrases I penned
ushered in
A school of thought
A new philosophy
On how to think
On how to live
And most importantly, how to love
How to love the Creator, His creation, you,
and one another
Simultaneously

And if this were a simulation,
I believe I'd been preprogrammed to author

I've said it before, and I'll say it again
Without the words here on this page I could
not fare

To imagine a world without poetry, I
wouldn't dare
A hellscape

Jorge Luis Borges said, "I have always
imagined Paradise will be a kind of library."
And I believe

A God who can be found in the Greatness
and in the nuance
Would delight in such mystery
That even the blind could revel in
And be blind no more
A mystery so large
That thousands of years and 7,117 languages
later we still can't quite explain

I believe that's why poetry exists
Because we poets say "Sure, I can't fully
explain this…"
But if I pull a bit from every catharsis,
image, and person I experience,
Then maybe I can string them
Into soliloquy
and entice any listeners who dare to see
Beyond only what can just be seen
But felt with the heart
Stirred within the Spirit
And tickled in the mind.

I liken poetry to a playground
An exploratory search
A fun introspection
An adventure
I see-saw between conclusiveness
I swing along the winds of parallelism
To find myself climbing the bars of
metacognition

Who has such time to think— I am far too
busy playing with thought.

MASTERPIECE
The writer in Ecclesiastes says
Everything is meaningless
Everything is vanity
without God.
But may I submit to you that
With God,
Everything is worship?

Have you ever noticed that blades of grass
moving in the wind look like they're
praising?
Have you ever noticed the sunflower
struggling against the elements to push its
way to the Light?
Have you ever noticed the pattern in tree
stumps resembles a fingerprint?

Like many of us
Such masterpieces.
We are art in the hands of the Creator.
We are artists that He teaches to use His
paintbrushes
to paint with colors like:
Love, Joy,
Peace, Patience,
Kindness, Goodness,
Faithfulness.

I draw artistic inspiration
from the best creation,

the universe,
made by the best Creator.

If life is like a puzzle,
then these are my pieces.
These poems are my peace.
If this is the Lord's work,
then these are,
I Am,
His masterpiece.

ABOUT THE AUTHOR

Kamille Elizabeth is a poet and author hailing from Winston-Salem, NC. She is passionate about education and teaching the importance of faith, positive self-talk, therapy, and creating art as a means of overcoming trauma and taking back control of one's mental wellness. Her debut poetry collection titled <u>To Bloom in the Valley</u> details her coming of age journey of finding faith, battling depression, honoring her Black American heritage, advocating for abuse survivors & victims, and discovering healing through art, introspection, love, & nature.